Little Hands Can Too

crafts for young children

Anita Reith Stohs
illustrated by Gordon Willman

CONCORDIA PUBLISHING HOUSE · SAINT LOUIS

To Immanuel's children: Andrew, Matthew, Miriam, Christopher, Justin, Katie, Matthew V., Michelle, Megan, Rachel, Shannon, and Timmy, with thanks for showing me some of the wonderful things little hands can do.

Copyright © 1994 Concordia Publishing House
3558 S. Jefferson Avenue, St. Louis, MO 63118-3968
Manufactured in the United States of America

Teachers may reproduce pages for classroom use only.

6 7 8 9 10 11 12 13 14   11 10 09 08 07 06 05 04

Contents

Note to Teachers and Parents 5

Old Testament

"Let There Be Light": *Straw Blowing*...................6

What a Wonderful World: *Stand-up Nature Collage*...................7

Feel God's World: *Texture Box* 8

God's Continuing Creation: *Seed Plaque*...................9

A Floating Zoo: *Sticker Collage* 10–11

Rainbow of Promise: *Yarn Drawing*...................12

Father Abraham's Stars: *Sprinkle Art*...................13

God's Angel Helpers: *Handprint Picture* 14–15

Joseph's Wonderful Coat: *Tube Puppet* 16

Living in God's Love: *Handprint Family*...................17

Moses in the Basket: *Nutshell Puppet*...................18

Food from the Lord: *Heated-Crayon Plaque* 19

Samuel's New Robe: *Fabric Collage* 20–21

Praise the Lord: *Yarn Lacing* 22–23

David's Sheep: *Paper-Plate Mask* 24

A Temple for the Lord: *Shape Collage*...................25

Fed by the Birds: *Feather Painting*...................26

New Testament

Good News Angel: *Tube Puppet* 27

Little Town of Bethlehem: *Window Drawing* 28

Follow That Star: *Craft-Sticks Ornament*...................29

A Gift to Give: *Decorated Gift Bag*...................30

Jesus Is Born: *Yarn Ornament* 31

Joy to the World: *Dough Ornament*...................32

How Jesus Lived: *Milk-Carton House* 33

Going to Church: *Shape Book* 34–35

I Follow Jesus: *Foot Printing* 36

Jesus Loves the Little Children: *Heart Tree* 37

Cared for by God: *Shredded-Wheat Nest* 38

Jesus Stops a Storm: *Finger Painting* 39

A Parade for the King: *Colored-Tape Collage* 40–41

Praise the Lord with Your Hands: *Shaving-Cream Painting* 42

He Died for Me: *Block Stamping* 43

Jesus Lives: *Pinch-Pot Tomb* 44

Easter Garden: *Torn-Paper Collage* 45

The Nets Were Full: *Fingerprint Fish* 46

Ascended into Heaven: *Whipped-Soap Painting* 47

Flame of the Spirit: *Sponge Printing* 48

Note to Teachers and Parents

This book suggests creative activities for young children for Bible stories often taught in preschool and lower elementary classes. The purpose of this book is to help children actively experience God's great love for them as revealed to us in stories from His own Word. Each finished craft item will also serve as a reminder of the Bible story and the message it shares.

Though activities have been designed for use with specific Bible stories, they are open-ended enough to allow children to interpret the project in their own unique ways. Suggestions at the end of the activities provide other ways the projects can be done. God is a creative God. We, as teachers, should allow His little children to be creative too.

Preschool children may find some activities difficult. Offer only as much help as needed. Be sure to supervise closely activities that use small objects, to prevent children from choking and other injury.

Patterns are provided for use with the very young and for the convenience of teachers and parents who need them. However, children should be encouraged to draw their own shapes as soon as they are able to do so. Allow children to fill in the shapes according to their own developmental level. Young children in the "manipulative" stage (ages 2–4) will scribble. Older children who have reached the "symbolic" stage (ages 4–7) will develop ways to use symbolic lines and shapes to express their ideas and feelings. As children work, always remember that the goal in child art is process, not product.

May God bless your teaching as you use these craft activities to help little children grow in joy, knowledge, love, and faith in their loving Lord and Savior.

Anita Reith Stohs

"Let There Be Light"

BIBLE STORY

Creation (Genesis 1)

MATERIALS

Thick, yellow tempera paint

Black construction paper

Spoon

Drinking straw

Glitter in shaker

Cardboard box

WAYS BIG HANDS CAN HELP

1. Set out a sheet of paper and a straw for each child.

2. Ask the children to cover their eyes. Say that once everything was dark; then God made the light. As the children uncover their eyes, talk about the many things we see in God's good light.

3. Put a spoonful of paint in the center of each sheet of paper.

4. Carefully watch so the children do not suck paint into the straw.

5. Supervise the children as they lay their wet, straw-blown painting inside a cardboard box and shake glitter onto it.

6. Help children transport projects to a "safe" place to dry.

LITTLE HANDS AT WORK

1. Blow paint around the paper with a drinking straw.

2. Lay the painting on the bottom of a box.

3. Shake glitter onto the painting.

4. Tell what they most like to see in God's good light.

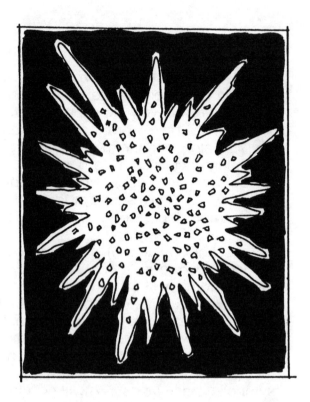

OTHER IDEAS

1. Omit glitter, use only tempera paint.

2. Show how a prism breaks light into different colors. Blow different "rainbow" colors over the paper.

3. Use bright, fluorescent colors for the activity.

4. Make celebration pictures to go with other lessons.

5. Write "Let There Be Light" on the picture.

What a Wonderful World

BIBLE STORY

Creation (Genesis 1)

MATERIALS

Self-hardening play dough
   1 part water
   ½ part flour
   1 part salt
Saucepan
Wooden spoon
Airtight container
Objects found in nature
Baking sheet

WAYS BIG HANDS CAN HELP

1. Mix the ingredients for play dough in a saucepan. Cook and stir over low heat until thick. Remove from heat and let cool. Divide the dough into large balls, one for each child. Store in an airtight container until needed.

2. Introduce the story by saying, "God made a wonderful world filled with many wonderful things. Let's take a walk to discover some of them!"

3. Take children on a walk outside your church, school, or home. Show them how to stick the small objects they find into their play-dough ball. Take care that the children do not pick up sharp or poisonous objects.

4. Designate a suitable place where the projects can dry.

LITTLE HANDS AT WORK

1. Take a walk in God's wonderful world. Look for small objects from nature, such as leaves, twigs, rocks, bark, feathers, or shells to stick into your play-dough ball.

2. When you return, talk about what you found. Set the play dough on a baking sheet to harden. When dry, save the play dough to remind you of the wonderful world God has made for you.

OTHER IDEAS

1. Add several drops of food coloring to the play-dough mixture before cooking.

2. Omit the walk. Provide or ask the children to bring in objects from nature ahead of time.

3. Have children gather nature objects in a bag. Then glue the objects to a piece of cardboard or Styrofoam. Use a paste made of equal amounts of flour and salt mixed with water.

Texture Box

Feel God's World

BIBLE STORY

Creation (Genesis 1)

MATERIALS

Empty tissue box

White paper

Scissors

Crayons

Glue

Box containing objects of various texture from nature

WAYS BIG HANDS CAN HELP

1. Gather objects from nature that have different textures.

2. Trim paper to fit around an empty tissue box.

3. Peel paper off some crayons.

4. Set out the crayons, glue, tissue boxes, and trimmed paper.

5. Explain that *texture* means how something feels—hard, soft, rough, or smooth. Have the children take turns picking out an object from your "nature box" and telling how it feels. Say, "Let's make our own nature boxes to remind us of the many different textures God has made."

LITTLE HANDS AT WORK

1. Pick out several objects with different textures from the "nature" box.

2. Place your paper over these objects. Rub over the paper with the side of a crayon.

3. Glue the paper around the box.

4. Put your objects in the box. Take out the objects, one at a time, and tell what it feels like.

5. Use your texture box to collect more objects with different textures, all made by God.

OTHER IDEAS

1. Use other kinds of boxes such as cereal boxes, cracker boxes, and milk cartons.

2. Use your box for a "texture game." Let someone reach in your box, hold an object, and guess what it is by how it feels.

3. Omit the rubbings. Go on a nature walk and let children pick their own objects of different textures to put into their boxes.

4. Write "Thank God for Texture" on the box.

God's Continuing Creation

BIBLE STORY

Creation (Genesis 1)

Caution: Never leave children unattended while working with very small objects. This activity works best with children age five and older.

MATERIALS

Dried beans, seeds, and/or nuts

Empty plastic container

Dough paste
   1 part salt
   1 part flour
Water

Shallow bowl

Spoon

Paper plate

Hole punch

Yarn

WAYS BIG HANDS CAN HELP

1. Set out bags of dried beans, seeds, and/or nuts. (Use large seeds from pumpkins or sunflowers, kidney and lima beans.)

2. Mix flour and salt in a shallow bowl. Stir in enough water to make a dough paste.

3. Provide a plastic container and a paper plate for each child. Punch a hole at the top of the plate.

4. Show some of the beans, seeds, and/or nuts. Ask what will happen if each is planted. Explain that God uses seeds to make new plants grow. Talk about how God blesses us with plants (food, beauty, medicines).

5. Place some dough paste and a spoon on each plate.

6. Help the children string a piece of yarn through the hole for a hanger.

LITTLE HANDS AT WORK

1. Pick out the beans, seeds, or nuts you wish to use. Place them in a plastic container.

2. Use the spoon to spread the dough paste over the plate.

3. Scatter the seeds, beans, or nuts over the plate.

4. Hang up the plate when it is dry to remind you how God makes new plants grow in the wonderful world He provides for you.

OTHER IDEAS

1. Instead of a paper plate use a Styrofoam plate or tray, or part of an egg carton.

2. Have children use plastic lids to sort beans or nuts before pasting.

3. Encourage older children to create a design with their seeds, beans, or nuts.

A Floating Zoo

BIBLE STORY

Noah (Genesis 6–9)

MATERIALS

Ark pattern (see page 11)

Animal stickers

Crayons

Scissors

WAYS BIG HANDS CAN HELP

1. Duplicate the ark shape. Cut out or help the children cut out the shape.

2. Set out crayons and stickers.

3. Say, "The wind blew and the rain poured down, but Noah and the animals stayed warm and dry inside the big ark." Put animal stickers on the ark shape to show how God kept the animals safe from the great flood. Ask, "How does God keep you safe?"

4. If needed, assist young children in removing stickers from their backing.

LITTLE HANDS AT WORK

1. Glue animal stickers onto the ark shape.

2. Use crayons to add other details (Noah and his family, food for the trip, other animals not shown on the stickers).

OTHER IDEAS

1. Have the children draw their favorite animals inside the ark.

2. Glue the ark to colored construction paper. Add paper details, such as water, raindrops, clouds, etc.

3. Let the children cut out their own ark outline.

4. Cut the ark shape from brown construction paper or a paper bag.

5. Enlarge the ark pattern. Instead of cutting it out, have the children draw and color wind, rain, and waves onto the space around it.

Pattern for "A Floating Zoo"

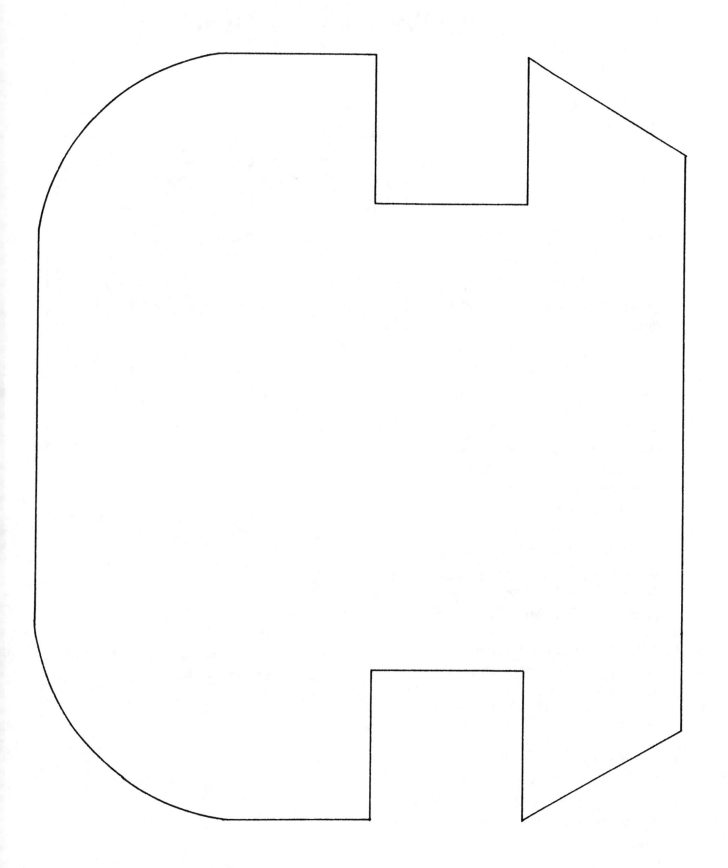

Rainbow of Promise

BIBLE STORY

Noah (Genesis 6–9)

MATERIALS

Sandpaper

Yarn of several rainbow colors

WAYS BIG HANDS CAN HELP

1. Cut lengths of yarn, each color to the size needed for a rainbow.

2. Set out sandpaper, one sheet for each child.

3. Say, "What do you think about when you see a rainbow? When Noah saw a rainbow, he thought about God's promise to never again send such a great flood. Use yarn to make your own rainbow on the sheet of sandpaper." (Yarn will adhere to sandpaper. It can be removed and used again.) Accept all shapes the rainbow may take, from straight across to circular.

4. While the children work, talk about other promises God gives to us, especially His promise of salvation in Jesus.

LITTLE HANDS AT WORK

Make a rainbow shape by pressing pieces of yarn onto sandpaper. Let your rainbow remind you of God's promises to you.

OTHER IDEAS

1. Let the children make a "rainbow picture" by swirling on the yarn as they desire. (This is most appropriate for young children.)

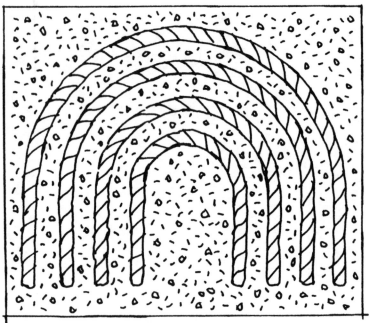

2. Allow children to save their rainbow by gluing it to the sandpaper.

3. Use liquid tempera to paint a background onto the sandpaper.

4. Make a sandpaper ark. Use yarn to make animals inside it.

5. Save your yarn and sandpaper to illustrate other Bible stories.

Father Abraham's Stars

BIBLE STORY

God's Covenant with Abraham (Genesis 15:1–6; 17:1–8)

MATERIALS

Construction paper (black or dark blue)

White glue

Cotton swabs

Salt in shaker

Plastic lid

Cardboard box

WAYS BIG HANDS CAN HELP

1. Place a saltshaker by a cardboard box.

2. Set out a sheet of construction paper, a plastic lid, and two cotton swabs for each child.

3. Pour a little glue onto each plastic lid. Set two cotton swabs by it.

4. Ask, "How many stars do you think there are in the sky? God promised to give Abraham as many children, grandchildren, and great-grandchildren as the stars. One of those children would be the Savior of the world. Let's make a star picture to remind us of that promise."

LITTLE HANDS AT WORK

1. Use the cotton swab to dot glue over the sheet of construction paper.

2. Place the paper in the cardboard box. Sprinkle salt over it.

3. Shake off excess salt and remove the picture.

OTHER IDEAS

1. Sprinkle on glitter, soap powder, sugar, sand, or colored rice instead of salt.

2. Dot white glue onto white paper. Let dry and cover with a dark, watercolor wash.

3. Draw stars with metallic crayons.

4. One of Abraham's descendants was Jesus. Make one star bigger to represent the promised Savior.

5. Sing the song "Father Abraham" as you work. Consider singing the words "Father Abraham saw many stars; Many stars saw Father Abraham" for the first two lines.

God's Angel Helpers

BIBLE STORY

Jacob's Dream (Genesis 28:10–22)

MATERIALS

Dark blue burlap

Styrofoam tray

Scissors

Hole punch

Yarn

White tempera paint

White glue

Colored glue

White felt

Dishwashing liquid

Paper towels

Paper plate

WAYS BIG HANDS CAN HELP

1. Set out colored glue. (Make your own by adding food coloring to a squeeze bottle of white glue.)

2. Cut burlap pieces to fit inside the Styrofoam trays.

3. Punch a hole in the top of each tray. Tie a small piece of yarn through the hole for a hanger.

4. Cut triangles and circles from white felt for the angel shapes (see patterns on page 15).

5. Prepare several stamp pads. Fold two paper towels and place them on a paper plate. Pour white tempera paint over them. Then pour a little dishwashing liquid over them for easy cleanup.

6. Say, "Can you think of a time you were afraid at night? God and His angels are with you, just as they were with Jacob long ago. Let's make a picture for your room to remind you of this whenever you are afraid."

7. Designate a surface to lay the pictures while they dry.

LITTLE HANDS AT WORK

1. Press each hand into the white tempera paint. Spread your fingers and use your hands as stamps to paint angel wings on the burlap piece.

2. Glue the triangle and circle onto the burlap piece for the angel's body and head. Use colored glue to add details to the angel and background.

3. Glue the burlap picture to the tray. Decorate the edges of the tray with colored glue.

God's Angel Helpers

OTHER IDEAS

1. With an adult's help, use colored glue to write "God's Angels Guard (name of child)" on the burlap.

2. Glue metallic stars onto the burlap background.

3. Use glitter pen instead of colored glue.

4. Sprinkle glitter over the entire picture before the glue and paint dry.

5. Glue on metallic sequins.

6. Glue on yarn for hair and other details. Add yarn along the edges of the tray for a decorative outline.

7. Use a paper doily instead of white felt.

8. Omit felt. Have the children outline the angel with colored glue or a glitter pen.

9. Outline the angel for younger children, and have them glue in pieces of a paper doily, lace, or metallic ribbon.

10. Make a burlap banner instead of a picture.

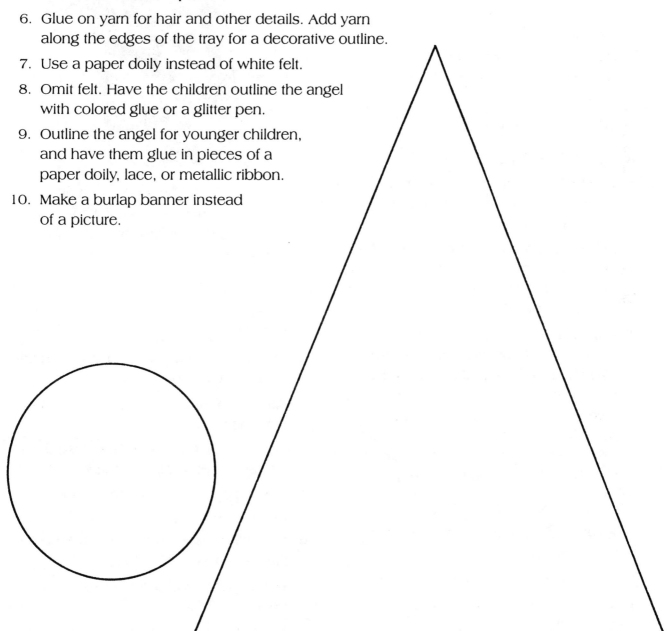

Joseph's Wonderful Coat

BIBLE STORY

Joseph's Coat (Genesis 37:3–36)

MATERIALS

Watercolors

Paintbrush

Containers of water

White construction paper

Scissors

Glue

White cardboard tube

WAYS BIG HANDS CAN HELP

1. Use the end of the cardboard tube to trace circles onto white paper. Cut out the circles.

2. Set out a cardboard tube for each child, as well as the paper circles, watercolors, brushes, and containers of water, for rinsing the paintbrushes.

3. Ask, "Have your parents ever given you some clothes you thought were especially beautiful? Once Jacob gave his son Joseph a very special coat to show love to him. Let's make a tube puppet for Joseph. Paint the tube to show what you think Joseph's wonderful coat looked like. Then make a face for your puppet."

LITTLE HANDS AT WORK

1. Paint pretty designs on the outside of a tube. Let it dry.

2. Paint Joseph's face on a paper circle.

3. When dry, glue the face towards the top of the tube.

4. Pretend your puppet is Joseph. Tell the story of what happened to him after his father gave him the beautiful coat. How did God show love to Joseph? How does God show His love for you?

OTHER IDEAS

1. Use brown cardboard tubes covered with white paper.

2. Use markers, crayons, or tempera paint to color in the coat.

3. Attach a happy-face sticker for the puppet's face.

4. Make a tube puppet to show Joseph as Pharaoh's second-in-command.

5. Use a crayon or marker to draw in Joseph's face.

6. Cut a circle face from skin-colored construction paper.

7. Use paper to add other details to the puppet.

8. Let children who can do so, cut out and draw their own circle face.

Living in God's Love

BIBLE STORY

Joseph Reassures His Brothers (Genesis 50:15–19)

MATERIALS

Red construction paper

Scissors

Crayons

Glue

Decorative fabric trim (lace, ribbon, etc.)

WAYS BIG HANDS CAN HELP

1. Cut out a red construction-paper heart for each child.
   a. Fold red paper in half.
   b. Cut half of a heart shape on the fold as indicated in the diagram. Unfold.

2. Cut fabric trim into pieces that children can easily handle (approximately 2–3").

3. Set out paper hearts, fabric trim, crayons, glue, and scissors.

4. Say, "Sometimes it's hard to forgive, isn't it? The Bible story of Joseph and his brothers reminds us that God's love makes us willing to forgive one another. Let's make a picture to show how our family is happy to forgive and to be forgiven."

5. Some children may need help with counting and tracing around their fingers.

LITTLE HANDS AT WORK

1. Count the number of people in your family. Place one hand in the center of the heart shape. Use a crayon to trace around your fingers. Draw one finger for each member of your family.

2. Color in faces and hair for each family member.

3. Cut and glue on pieces of fabric trim to decorate your heart.

OTHER IDEAS

1. Let children (if they are able) cut out the heart and trace around their fingers on their own.

2. Omit finger outlines and draw shapes for each member of the family.

3. Cover the heart with clear contact paper. Use washable markers for drawing. Wash off and save the hearts for other lessons that emphasize the love we share from God.

4. Write on the heart, "The (family name) Family Shares God's Love."

5. Glue on pieces cut from a paper doily.

Moses in the Basket

BIBLE STORY

The Birth of Moses (Exodus 2:1–10)

Warning: Due to the risk of choking, do not allow preschool children to eat the peanuts. Never leave children unattended during this activity.

MATERIALS

English walnut shell

Whole peanut shells

Fine-tipped marker

Fabric scraps

Scissors

Glue

WAYS BIG HANDS CAN HELP

1. Cut a strip of fabric to cover half of each peanut shell.

2. Provide a walnut shell, markers, a peanut shell, and glue for each child.

3. Ask, "What kind of bed did you have when you were a baby? Moses once had a basket in a big river for a bed. Let's make a little puppet to help us tell the story of how God took care of Baby Moses."

LITTLE HANDS AT WORK

1. Use the marker to draw a face and hair on one end of the peanut.

2. Glue the fabric strip around the bottom half of the peanut for a baby blanket.

3. Set the peanut inside the walnut shell.

4. Act out the story of what happened to Moses when his mother put him and his basket in the water. Tell about ways God takes care of you.

OTHER IDEAS

1. Float the walnut boat in a pan of water.

2. Glue Moses into his shell boat.

3. Make peanut puppets for Moses' mother, Miriam, and Pharaoh's daughter. Stand them up in balls of play dough.

Food from the Lord

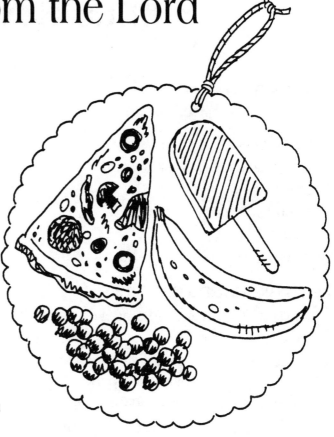

BIBLE STORY

Manna in the Wilderness (Exodus 16)

MATERIALS

Paper plate

Crayons

Oven

Cookie sheet

Hole punch

Yarn

WAYS BIG HANDS CAN HELP

1. Punch a hole in the rim of each paper plate.

2. Set out crayons.

3. Ask, "What is your favorite food? Do you know where it comes from? Long ago God sent His people a special food called manna. Let's make a plaque to help you remember that your food today still comes from God."

4. Set the oven to "warm." "Bake" the paper-plate plaques several minutes to set their color.

5. Help the children string yarn through the hole for a hanger.

LITTLE HANDS AT WORK

1. Draw and color your favorite foods on a paper plate.

2. Place your plate on a cookie sheet.

3. Talk with your helper about how God gives you the food you drew on the plate.

4. Hang up the plate as a reminder that your food comes from God.

OTHER IDEAS

1. Instead of heating crayon drawings, put stickers of different kinds of food on the plate.

2. Act out the story. Use the plate for gathering snack crackers.

3. Write "(Name of child)'s Food Comes from the Lord" around the rim of the plate.

4. Write the words of a familiar table prayer around the rim of the plate.

5. Cut fringes around the edges of a sheet of construction paper for a place mat. Glue on the plate, a napkin, and plastic dinnerware. Hang up your display.

6. Make food from colored, self-drying play dough to put on the plate.

7. Omit heating the plaque.

Fabric Collage
Samuel's New Robe

BIBLE STORY

Samuel (1 Samuel 2:18–21)

MATERIALS

Construction paper (skin color)

Scissors

Fabric scraps

Glue

Crayons

WAYS BIG HANDS CAN HELP

1. Duplicate the outline of Samuel on page 21.

2. Trace the outline of Samuel onto a sheet of skin-colored construction paper. Cut out shapes for children unable to do so.

3. Cut fabric scraps to a size the children can easily handle.

4. Set out enough crayons and glue for all to use.

5. Ask the children to tell how they got their newest coat. Tell them that when Samuel lived and served God in the temple, his mother made him a new coat each year. Have the children pretend to help Hannah make Samuel's newest robe. Talk about ways they can serve God in church, in school, and at home.

LITTLE HANDS AT WORK

1. Cut out the outline of Samuel.

2. Draw Samuel's face, hair, and sandals on the picture.

3. Spread glue over the coat. Stick on pieces of fabric.

OTHER IDEAS

1. Let older children draw their own outlines and cut their own fabric pieces.

2. Let children (age five and older) glue on buttons and fabric trim.

3. Cut the outline from poster board or cardboard for a stand-up figure.

4. Cover the coat with scraps of wrapping paper or construction paper of various designs and colors.

5. Paint the coat with watercolors. Consider wetting the coat outline before dabbing on the paint.

6. Use the collage when studying the story of Joseph and his beautiful coat.

Pattern for "Samuel's New Robe"

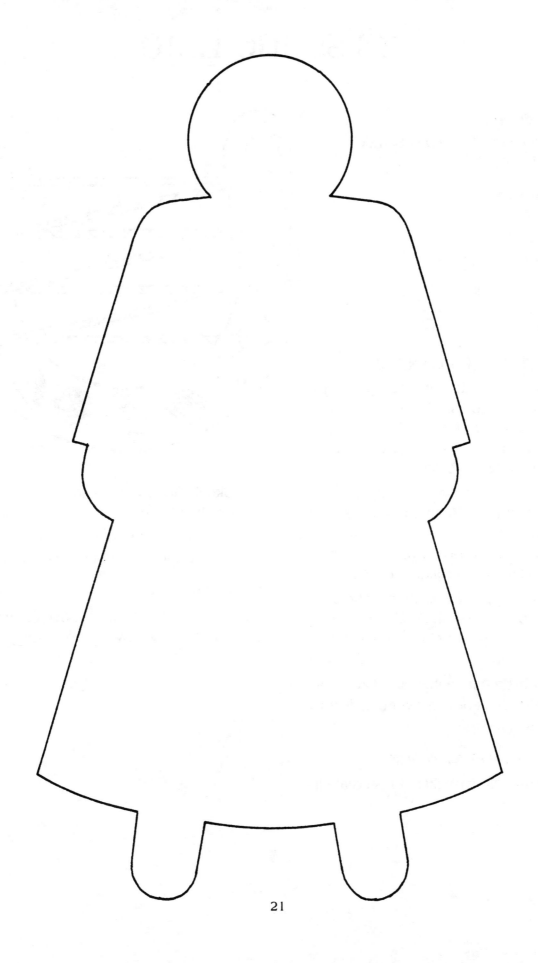

21

Praise the Lord

BIBLE STORY

David Plays His Harp (1 Samuel 16:14–23)

MATERIALS

Poster board

Hole punch

Crayons or markers

Yarn

Tape

Scissors

WAYS BIG HANDS CAN HELP

1. Duplicate and cut out the harp pattern found on page 23. Trace and cut out harp shapes from poster board, one for each child. Punch holes along inside of each harp as indicated.

2. For each harp cut a piece of yarn approximately 2' long. Knot one end of the yarn and wrap tape around the other end. Help the children get started by pulling the yarn through the first hole.

3. Say, "David played his harp as he sang songs of praise to the Lord. You can too. Lace the harp and 'play' it as you sing praises to God."

4. Help children tape the yarn down when finished. (Accept whatever direction the "harp strings" run.)

LITTLE HANDS AT WORK

1. Use crayons or markers to decorate the harp.

2. Poke the taped end of the yarn through each hole to make strings on the harp.

3. Pretend to play your harp as you sing your favorite song of praise to God.

OTHER IDEAS

Enlarge the harp shape, or have older children draw their own harp shape.

Pattern for "Praise the Lord"

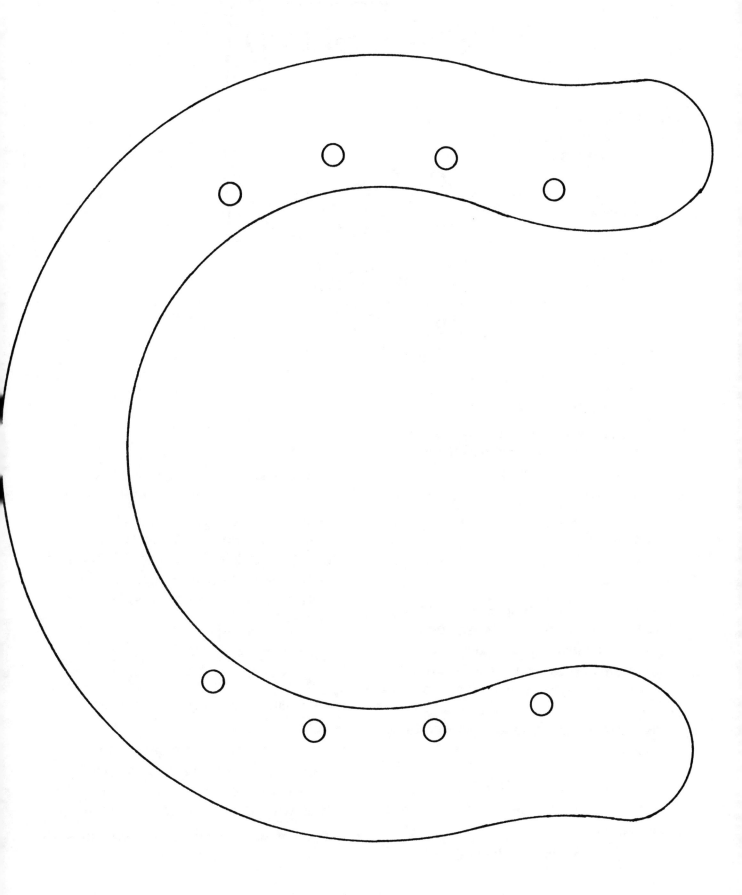

David's Sheep

BIBLE STORY

David Cares for His Sheep (1 Samuel 16:11; 17:34–35)

MATERIALS

Paper plate

Scissors

Elastic cord

Cotton balls

Glue

Markers or crayons

White construction paper

WAYS BIG HANDS CAN HELP

1. Cut eye holes in each paper plate.

2. Duplicate the pattern provided for the sheep's ear. Cut two ears for each mask from white construction paper.

3. Poke small holes in each side of the mask. Cut a piece of elastic cord for each mask.

4. Provide glue, cotton balls, and markers or crayons.

5. Say, "David was a shepherd boy who took good care of his father's sheep. When his sheep were in danger, God gave David great courage and strength to protect his sheep. How does God protect you? What does God help you to do? Let's make masks and pretend to be David's sheep."

LITTLE HANDS AT WORK

1. Draw the sheep's nose and mouth. Glue on the ears.

2. Glue cotton balls onto the paper plate.

3. Have an adult help you tie on the elastic cord.

4. Wear the mask and pretend to be a sheep. With some friends, take turns being David, leading his flock and taking good care of his sheep. Remember that God leads you and takes good care of you too.

OTHER IDEAS

1. Use when teaching Psalm 23.

2. Use with Jesus' story about the Good Shepherd.

3. Glue a craft stick to the back of the paper plate to make a stick puppet. This works especially well with young children who do not wish to wear a mask.

4. Use yarn instead of elastic cord. Staple or tape it to the paper plate.

A Temple for the Lord

BIBLE STORY

Solomon's Temple (1 Kings 6)

MATERIALS

Construction paper

Wallpaper samples

Scissors

Glue

WAYS BIG HANDS CAN HELP

1. Cut wallpaper into pieces that older children will be able to cut with a scissors. Cut smaller strips and shapes for younger children to use.

2. Set out glue, scissors, and a background sheet of construction paper for each child.

3. Tell the children that Solomon took seven years to build a beautiful temple-church for the Lord. Ask them to make a picture to show what this beautiful temple might have looked like. Talk about ways we can praise God in church.

LITTLE HANDS AT WORK

1. Pick out wallpaper shapes to use for your picture or cut pieces of wallpaper into smaller shapes.

2. Glue the wallpaper shapes onto the paper. Make a beautiful temple-church to praise the Lord.

OTHER IDEAS

1. Incorporate other materials into the picture such as fabric, aluminum foil, or plastic wrap. Glue heavier objects onto a piece of cardboard or poster board.

2. Use colorful pieces of construction paper instead of wallpaper.

3. Have children make a picture of their own church.

4. Use crayons or markers to add details, such as Solomon and his people worshiping in the temple.

5. Ask children to make the kind of temple Solomon might build if he lived today.

Fed by the Birds

BIBLE STORY

Elijah (1 Kings 17:1–6)

MATERIALS

Picture of a crow

Drawing paper

Tempera paint (black and at least one other color)

Dishwashing liquid

Feather

WAYS BIG HANDS CAN HELP

1. Mix some dishwashing liquid with tempera paint to aid in cleanup.

2. Set out paper and feathers.

3. Invite the children to describe what a crow looks like. Show a picture of a crow. Explain that once God fed his servant Elijah with food brought by these big blackbirds, also called ravens. Tell the children that they will use a feather to paint a picture of these big crows bringing bread and meat to feed Elijah. Talk about ways God provides food for us.

LITTLE HANDS AT WORK

1. Dip the tip of a feather into black tempera and paint the blackbirds.

2. Use other colors to paint the food the birds are bringing to Elijah. Name some food that God gives to you.

OTHER IDEAS

1. Use watercolors to add Elijah and a brook to the picture.

2. Omit additional colors. Glue on pieces of flat, breakfast cereal for the food carried by the ravens.

3. Use sponges to stamp in the food brought by the ravens.

4. Draw Elijah and his food with markers or crayons.

5. Make a class mural with many ravens in the sky.

6. Sing the following song to the tune of "Sing a Song of Sixpence":

    Sing a song of sixpence, a pocket full of rye,
    Many, many blackbirds flying through the sky.
    When they find Elijah they open up their beak,
    Out drops bread and meat that God has sent for him to eat.

Tube Puppet

Good News Angel

BIBLE STORY

The Annunciation (Luke 1:26–38)

MATERIALS

White cardboard tube

Cupcake liners

Glue

Marker

Paper doily

Scissors

Yellow yarn (optional)

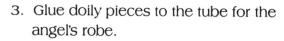

WAYS BIG HANDS CAN HELP

1. Cut doilies into 2–3″ pieces.

2. Cut yellow yarn into pieces that fit around the top of the cardboard tubes (optional). Help the children glue on yarn for a halo.

3. Set out tubes, glue, markers, and scissors.

4. Allow children the freedom to come up with their own way to make the angel wings from cupcake liners. One idea is to fold the liners in half before gluing them, but other options are possible.

5. Tell the children that God sent a "Good News" angel to tell Mary that our Savior, Jesus, would soon be born. Say that they can make their own "Good News" angel to remind others that Jesus' birthday is coming soon.

LITTLE HANDS AT WORK

1. Use markers to draw an angel face and hair on one end of the cardboard tube.

2. Glue the yarn around the top of the tube for a halo (optional).

3. Glue doily pieces to the tube for the angel's robe.

4. Flatten two cupcake liners. Use them to make the angel's wings.

5. Use the angel puppet to tell others that Jesus' birthday is coming.

OTHER IDEAS

1. Use brown cardboard tubes. Cover them with white paper prior to the activity.

2. Use metallic cupcake liners and metallic paper doilies.

3. Use pieces of tinsel or garland for the angel's hair.

4. Let older children glue on ribbon, glitter, or sequins.

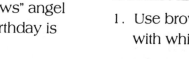

Little Town of Bethlehem

BIBLE STORY

Jesus Is Born (Luke 2:1–7)

MATERIALS

Glass wax

Window

Towels

WAYS BIG HANDS CAN HELP

1. Set out glass wax.

2. Ask the children, "Do you know the name of the town where Jesus was born? What do you think it looked like?" Have the children help you make a picture of Bethlehem on a glass window.

LITTLE HANDS AT WORK

1. Use your hands to help rub the wax over the glass.

2. Use your fingers to draw buildings for Bethlehem. Make a big star over the town to help the Wise Men find Baby Jesus. Draw the stable with Jesus, Mary, and Joseph. Let the picture remind you of the first Christmas when God sent Jesus to earth to be our Savior.

OTHER IDEAS

1. Draw different parts of the Christmas story on separate windows.

2. Add color to the picture by adding tempera paint to the wax.

3. When the time comes to remove the picture, let the children help you wipe it off with a towel.

Follow That Star

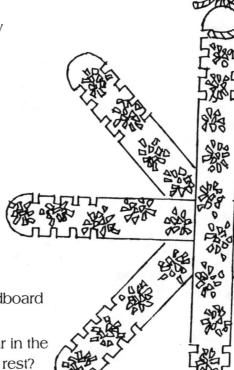

BIBLE STORY

The Visit of the Wise Men (Matthew 2:1–12)

MATERIALS

Notched craft sticks

Glue

Glitter in shaker

Shoe box

Thread

Scissors

WAYS BIG HANDS CAN HELP

1. Set out craft sticks and glue.

2. Place a glitter shaker inside a cardboard box.

3. Ask, "Have you ever seen one star in the sky that seemed brighter than the rest? Long ago, God put an especially bright star in the sky to lead the Wise Men to Jesus. Make your own bright star. Let it lead you to Jesus and remind you to worship Him."

4. Supervise the children as they glue their craft sticks and put glitter on them.

5. Designate a surface where the ornaments can dry.

6. Tie a loop of thread to one of the sticks for hanging.

LITTLE HANDS AT WORK

1. Create a star shape with four craft sticks. Glue the sticks together as you lay each on top of another, pointing it in a different direction. Let dry.

2. Dot glue on the star, place it in a shoe-box, and sprinkle glitter over it. Let dry.

3. Hang your star on your Christmas tree. Let it remind you to worship Jesus, your Savior.

OTHER IDEAS

1. Decorate the star with small pieces of metallic ribbon, stickers, sequins, or colored glue.

2. Use ordinary craft sticks instead of notched ones.

A Gift to Give

BIBLE STORY

The Visit of the Wise Men (Matthew 2:1–12)

MATERIALS

Paper bag

Markers or crayons

Religious Christmas stickers

Hole punch

Yarn

Gift item to put in bag

WAYS BIG HANDS CAN HELP

1. Punch two holes in each side of paper bags, as indicated in the diagram.

2. Cut a piece of yarn for each side of the bags. Poke the ends of the yarn piece through the holes and knot the ends.

3. Set out Christmas stickers and markers or crayons.

4. Tell the children, "Long ago the Wise Men brought gifts to Jesus. Today we will make a gift bag that we can give to someone to share our happiness at Jesus' birth."

LITTLE HANDS AT WORK

1. Use markers or crayons to color the bag.

2. Decorate the bag with stickers.

3. Fill the bag with a gift such as a picture, popcorn, "trail-mix," fruit, or craft. Give the gift to someone and share the Good News that Jesus, our Savior, is born.

OTHER IDEAS

1. Before punching holes into the bag, use strips of clear plastic tape to reinforce the sides, inside and outside.

2. Cut out pictures from Christmas cards to glue onto the bag.

3. Stamp Christmas designs onto the bag with holiday ink stamps or tempera paint and cookie cutters.

4. Make a special bag to hold Christmas cards at home.

5. Fill the bag with gift items for other children. Give the gifts to a church relief agency.

Jesus Is Born

BIBLE STORY

Birth of Jesus (Luke 2:1–20)

MATERIALS

Brightly colored yarn

Scissors

Liquid starch

Shallow bowls

Aluminum foil

WAYS BIG HANDS CAN HELP

1. Cut colorful yarn into different lengths, 3–6".

2. Pour liquid starch into shallow bowls.

3. Cut aluminum foil into 6" squares.

4. Say, "What if you had come with the shepherds to see Jesus the night He was born. How would you feel? Let's make an ornament that shows how happy we are that Jesus, our Savior, was born."

5. Designate a surface where ornaments can dry.

6. Tie loops of yarn to the ornaments for hanging.

LITTLE HANDS AT WORK

1. Pick out "happy" colors of yarn for your ornament.

2. Dip a piece of yarn into the liquid starch. Make a loop as you lay the yarn onto an aluminum-foil square. Dip and loop other pieces onto the foil, overlapping them as much as possible. Let dry.

OTHER IDEAS

1. Use thin white glue instead of liquid starch.

2. Older children may fill in spaces with cut or torn colored tissue paper.

3. Use a variety of yarns, especially those containing metallic threads.

4. Make ornaments in the shape of Christmas symbols.

Dough Ornament
Joy to the World

BIBLE STORY

Birth of Jesus (Luke 2:1–20)

MATERIALS

Baker's clay
  4 cups flour
  1 cup salt
  1½ cups water
Paper clips
Christmas cookie cutters
Rolling pin
Spatula
Baking sheet
Tempera paint mixed with white glue
Paintbrush

WAYS BIG HANDS CAN HELP

1. Combine the ingredients for the baker's clay. Knead the dough for five minutes. Divide into balls.

2. Set out cookie cutters, rolling pins, baking sheets, and paper clips.

3. Show the children some of the cookie shapes and ask, "What do these shapes remind you about the story of Jesus' birth?" Demonstrate how to roll out dough to about 1/4" thickness and stamp a shape with a cookie cutter. Insert a paper clip into the top of the shape for a hanger.

4. Help the children lift the dough shapes with a spatula and place them onto the cookie sheet. Bake the ornaments at 350 degrees up to one hour. Thinner ornaments will take less time. Mix tempera paint and white glue. Set out the paint and paintbrushes.

LITTLE HANDS AT WORK

1. Flatten the dough balls with a rolling pin.

2. Cut out shape with a cookie cutter.

3. Stick a paper clip into the top of the dough shape.

4. Place the shape into a baking sheet.

5. After baking and cooling, paint the ornament with the glue and tempera paint mixture.

6. Hang the ornament on your Christmas tree. Let it remind you of the coming of Baby Jesus, your Savior.

OTHER IDEAS

1. Decorate with markers or watercolor.

2. Before baking, press the tips of markers into the dough shapes to make patterns.

3. Make ornaments from self-drying play dough. Press colored plastic beads into the dough shapes.

How Jesus Lived

BIBLE STORY

Jesus at Nazareth (Matthew 2:23)

MATERIALS

Cardboard milk carton (half-gallon)
Brown paper
Glue
Crayons or markers
Green tissue paper
Scissors
Styrofoam tray

WAYS BIG HANDS CAN HELP

1. Trim off the tops of the milk cartons.

2. Cut a strip of brown paper to fit around each milk carton.

3. Cut green tissue into 2–3″ pieces.

4. Set out crayons or markers and Styrofoam trays.

5. Say, "Jesus grew up in a little town called Nazareth. He played and helped his parents just like you do. Jesus understands our feelings and concerns. He loves us and helps us at all times. Let's make a house like the one Jesus might have lived in as a boy."

LITTLE HANDS AT WORK

1. Use crayons or markers to draw a door and window(s) on the strip of brown paper. You might also draw Jesus, Mary, and Joseph.

2. Turn the milk carton upside down. Glue the paper around the carton.

3. Glue the milk carton to the Styrofoam tray.

4. Tear and crumple pieces of green tissue paper and glue them to the tray for grass and bushes.

5. Tell how your home is like or different from the house you made. Rejoice that Jesus knows and cares about you.

OTHER IDEAS

1. Use other colors of tissue paper to make a walk or rocks.

2. Substitute construction paper for colored tissue paper.

3. Glue the house onto a piece of cardboard colored with crayons or paint.

4. Cut the paper strip from a paper bag.

5. Make the house from a shoe box.

6. Glue items from nature such as bark, small rocks, and twigs onto the tray.

7. Cut a door and windows into the sides of the house.

8. Make and color a classroom "playhouse" made from a large cardboard box.

Going to Church

BIBLE STORY

Jesus in the Temple (Luke 2:41–52)

MATERIALS

White drawing paper

Crayons or markers

Scissors

Stapler

Fine-tipped marker

WAYS BIG HANDS CAN HELP

1. Duplicate the church pattern on page 35. Trace the pattern onto drawing paper, making several copies for each child. Cut out outlines for preschool children. Encourage older children to cut out their own outlines.

2. Write "(Name of child) Goes to Church" on one of the outlines to use as the cover of each child's book. Help young children to write their names in the title as needed.

3. Provide crayons or markers.

4. Say, "In the Bible we read about a time when Jesus was lost. His parents found him in the temple-church, talking with some of the teachers there. What do you do at your church? Let's make a book to show what you do in church to learn about God and to praise Him."

5. After children finish their pictures, use the fine-tipped marker to write on each page what they say about the picture. Help the children to staple the book together.

LITTLE HANDS AT WORK

1. Write your name on the cover page of the book. Draw in the church's door, window, and other details.

2. Draw and color pictures of things you do at church. Use as many pages as you wish.

3. Tell an adult what each picture is about.

4. Staple the book together with the cover page on top.

OTHER IDEAS

1. Cut the book's cover and pages from construction paper.

2. Enlarge the pattern and draw a picture of the church's interior.

3. Give young children only one outline. Encourage them to scribble happy "praise colors" over it.

4. Let older children outline their own church shape.

5. Bind pages together with a paper fastener or yarn.

Pattern for "Going to Church"

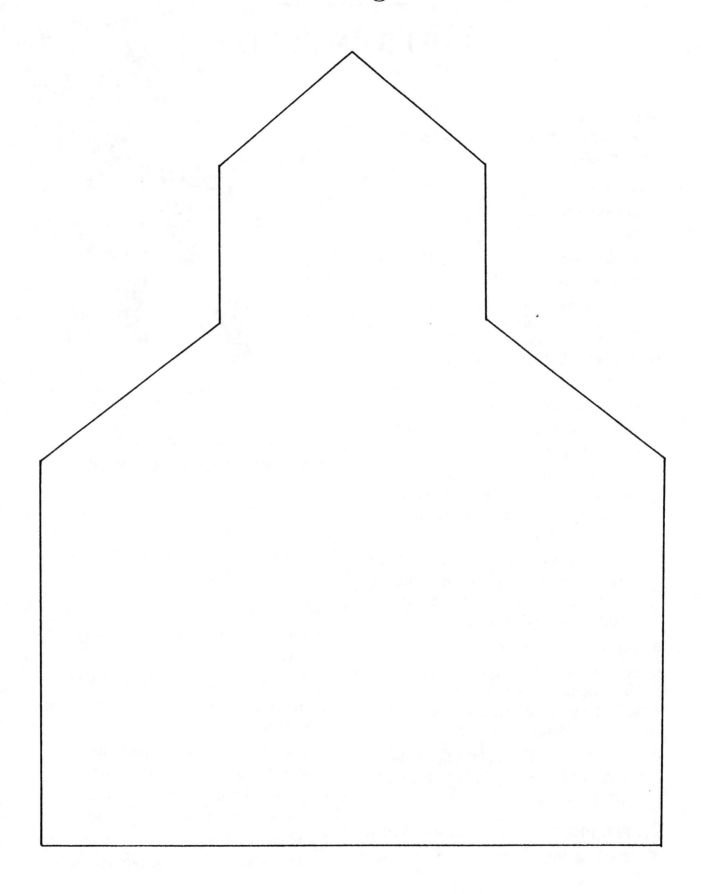

I Follow Jesus

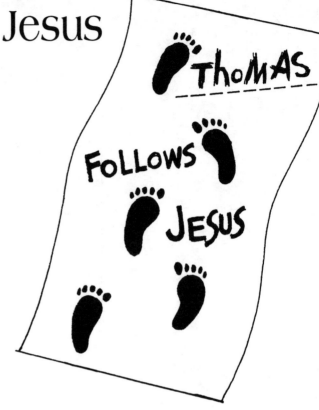

BIBLE STORY

Jesus Calls the First Disciples (Matthew 4:18–22)

MATERIALS

Tempera paint

Dishwashing liquid

Shallow pan

Butcher paper

Pan of soapy water and towels

Marker (optional)

WAYS BIG HANDS CAN HELP

1. Mix liquid tempera paint with dishwashing liquid for easy cleanup.

2. If done indoors, cover the floor with oilcloth or plastic.

3. Prepare a pan of soapy water and towels for cleanup. Have a second helper on hand to help the children clean off their feet.

4. Cut a large sheet of paper for each child. Write "(Name of child) Follows Jesus" on each sheet. (Draw a line where the child's name will go.)

5. Set out crayons or markers.

6. Say, "Jesus said, 'Follow Me,' to some fishermen, and they did. Let's make a footprint picture to remind us that Jesus calls us to follow Him too."

7. Help each child, one at a time, make a footprint picture. Caution: Paint will be slippery.

LITTLE FEET AND HANDS AT WORK

1. Take off your shoes. Dip your feet into the paint and walk on the butcher paper.

2. Step into the soapy water and clean off your feet.

3. Use a marker or crayon to write your name on the blank line.

Tell what you do when you "follow Jesus."

OTHER IDEAS

1. Instead of tempera paint, use finger-paint.

2. Make a class mural with many feet.

3. Stamp prints with old shoes on butcher paper.

4. Paint a set of large footprints as a reminder that Jesus "walks" with us.

5. Do the activity outdoors on a warm day. Use a garden hose to clean off feet.

6. Allow older children to paint their feet with different colors before printing.

Jesus Loves the Little Children

BIBLE STORY

Jesus and the Children (Mark 10:13–16)

MATERIALS

Red construction paper

Scissors

Markers or crayons

Yarn in different hair colors

Glue

Hole punch

Branch

Large jar

Pebbles or marbles

Tape

WAYS BIG HANDS CAN HELP

1. Cut a heart from red construction paper for each child; fold the paper in half, cut out half of the heart on the fold, then unfold it. Encourage older children to do this themselves.

2. Write "Jesus Loves Me" on one side of each heart. Make one more paper heart, write "Children Jesus Loves" on it and tape it to a jar.

3. Fill a large jar with marbles or pebbles. Insert a branch stripped of leaves or needles.

4. Punch a hole at the top of each heart. Loop a piece of yarn through the hole for a hanger.

5. Cut yarn into small pieces for hair.

6. Set out glue and crayons or markers.

7. Sing "Jesus Loves Me." Then say, "A heart shape reminds us of the love of Jesus, which we share with one another.

Let's make a 'heart tree' to help us remember that Jesus loves each of us."

LITTLE HANDS AT WORK

1. Draw your face onto a heart.

2. Glue on yarn for hair.

3. Hang your heart on the "heart tree."

OTHER IDEAS

1. Cut hearts from skin-colored construction paper.

2. Make additional hearts for other children loved by Jesus.

3. Use construction paper to add details to the hearts.

4. Cover the hearts with clear, adhesive plastic. Color with water-based marker. Wipe off and use for other Bible stories emphasizing Jesus' love.

Cared for by God

BIBLE STORY

Sermon on the Mount (Matthew 6:25–34)

MATERIALS

Shredded wheat

White glue

Mixing bowl

Metal spoon

Colored pipe cleaners

Scissors

Waxed paper

WAYS BIG HANDS CAN HELP

1. Mix shredded wheat with white glue to make a dough.

2. For older children, cut pipe cleaners into small segments for baby birds. Let the children come up with their own way to make bird shapes.

3. Cut waxed paper into squares for children to work on.

4. Make a nest and birds ahead of time to show the children. Talk about how well God takes care of little birds in their nests. Assure the children that God loves and cares for them even more.

LITTLE HANDS AT WORK

1. Crumble shredded wheat for the dough.

2. Mold the shredded-wheat dough into a nest.

3. Bend pipe cleaners into bird shapes.

4. Put the smaller pipe cleaners into the nest for the baby birds. Pretend to have the mother bird bring food to the babies,

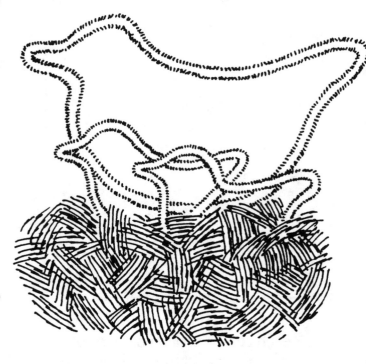

then have her sit in the nest to protect them.

5. Tell how God also gives you the home and food you need.

OTHER IDEAS

1. Combine different colorful pieces of pipe cleaners to make the birds.

2. Use the dough to make homes for other kinds of animals.

3. Mold a porcupine or hedgehog from the dough. Talk about how God protects them with their spiny covering.

4. Make nests from rice-cereal bars. Add candy eggs. Enjoy later for a snack.

Finger Painting

Jesus Stops a Storm

BIBLE STORY

Jesus Stills the Storm (Mark 4:35–41)

MATERIALS

Liquid starch

Blue powdered tempera paint in shaker

Glossy paper

WAYS BIG HANDS CAN HELP

1. Set out paper, liquid starch, and powdered tempera paint in a shaker.

2. Say, "One night Jesus and his friends were in a bad storm on a lake. Jesus told the storm, 'Be still,' and it stopped. Let's finger-paint two pictures to tell the story. First show the wild storm, then the quiet water."

3. Pour a little liquid starch on each sheet. Caution the children not to breathe in the powdered tempera paint. Have the children do one picture at a time.

4. Designate a surface where the pictures can dry.

LITTLE HANDS AT WORK

1. Move the liquid starch around and see what it does.

2. Sprinkle blue tempera paint over the starch and mix it in.

3. Use your fingers and hand to make wild waves in one picture.

4. Make another picture to show calm water.

5. When dry, use the two pictures to tell the story of how Jesus stopped the storm. Tell how Jesus uses His mighty power to protect you.

OTHER IDEAS

1. Older children may enjoy drawing in a boat with Jesus and His disciples over the pictures.

2. Sprinkle different colors onto the paper and mix them up.

3. Finger-paint a picture of the crossing of the Red Sea or other Bible stories that took place on water.

4. Use commercial finger paint or chocolate pudding.

5. Have the children finger-paint a storm from their experience when they were kept safe by God.

6. At the bottom of each picture, write down the child's explanation of what he or she has drawn.

A Parade for the King

BIBLE STORY

Jesus Enters Jerusalem (Matthew 21:1–11)

MATERIALS

Construction paper

Waxed paper

Green plastic tape

Scissors

Pencil

WAYS BIG HANDS CAN HELP

1. Duplicate and cut out the pattern on page 41.

2. Trace and cut out the pattern from construction paper for each child. Let older children trace/draw their own pattern for palm branches.

3. Cut a sheet of waxed paper for each child's working surface.

4. Cut and stick pieces of green tape to each sheet of waxed paper.

5. Ask the children, "What's it like to be at a parade? Have you ever waved at people in the parade as they rode or walked by? Once some children waved palm branches and sang 'Hosanna' as Jesus rode past. They did this to praise Jesus. Let's make our own branches to wave as we sing praises to Jesus like the children did on the first Palm Sunday."

LITTLE HANDS AT WORK

1. Pull off each piece of tape from the waxed paper and stick it onto the pattern to complete the palm leaf.

2. Wave your palm leaf as you march around the room singing a "Hosanna" song to Jesus.

OTHER IDEAS

1. Use different colors of tape to make the Hosanna palm.

2. Use colored masking tape instead of plastic tape.

3. Cut pieces of tape and stick them to the end of the table for children to pull off and use.

4. Allow older children to try cutting their own tape.

5. Instead of tape, stick on pieces of gummed ribbon. Or glue on pieces of yarn, construction paper, or colored tissue paper.

6. Scribble over the palm shape with green crayon or fingerpaint.

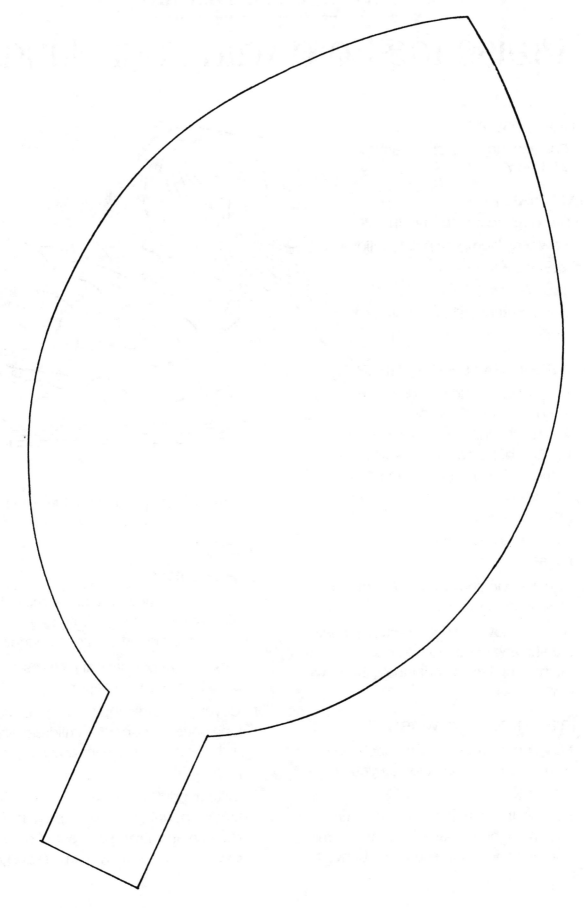

Praise the Lord with Your Hands

BIBLE STORY

Children Sing to Jesus (Matthew 21:14–17)

MATERIALS

Shaving cream (nonmentholated)

Powdered tempera paint (optional)

Washable table top

Tape player

Recording of children's songs

Paper towels

WAYS BIG HANDS CAN HELP

1. Say, "What would you do if Jesus came to your church? The Bible tells of a time when little children shouted 'Hosanna to the Son of David' to Jesus when He came to their temple-church. They praised Him with their voices. Let's praise Jesus right now with our hands."

2. Play a recording of children singing praises.

3. Squirt some shaving cream onto the table in front of each child.

4. Sprinkle powdered tempera paint over the shaving cream to add color. Be careful that children do not inhale the powder.

LITTLE HANDS AT WORK

1. Move your hands over the table, in time with the music. Sing along if you know the song.

2. Look at the beautiful and happy designs you made on the table. Let them remind you of the joy that Jesus' love brings to you. Help clean up the table with paper towels. Then wash your hands in the sink.

OTHER IDEAS

1. If you are concerned that some children will put the shaving cream into their mouths, try using chocolate pudding.

2. Finger-paint permanent pictures of praise onto glazed paper.

3. Cover your table top with an oilcloth or long sheet of paper for children to "paint" with the shaving cream and tempera paint.

4. Take a "print" from the colored shaving cream, pudding, or finger paint by momentarily laying a sheet of paper over it, then carefully lifting it up again.

Block Stamping

He Died for Me

BIBLE STORY

Jesus' Death (Matthew 27:32–56)

MATERIALS

White drawing paper

Wooden blocks

Liquid tempera paint

Paper plate

Paper towels

WAYS BIG HANDS CAN HELP

1. Prepare several "stamp pads," one for each 2–3 children. Fold two paper towels in half and place them on a paper plate. Pour liquid tempera paint onto the folded paper towels.

2. Set out blocks and drawing paper.

3. Say, "Jesus died on the cross to take away the sins of the whole world. He died for me and each one of you. Let's make cross pictures to remind us of how much Jesus loves us."

LITTLE HANDS AT WORK

1. Take a block and press it onto the "stamp pad." Then use the block to print a square on the paper. Repeat the printing until you make a cross shape.

2. Hang the cross in your room. Let it remind you of Jesus' love for you.

OTHER IDEAS

1. Stamp with finger paint or chocolate pudding.

2. Let children work on several additional "experimental" sheets.

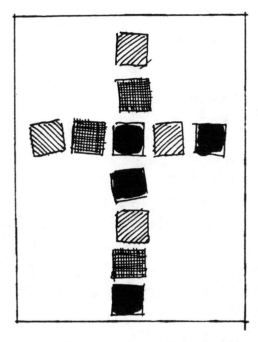

3. Stamp the cross onto construction paper.

4. Stamp different colors onto the page.

5. Use other objects found in the room for stamping.

6. If the children do not already know stanza 2 of "Jesus Loves Me, This I Know," teach it to them as they work.

Jesus loves me, He who died,
Heaven's gate to open wide;
He will wash away my sin,
Let His little child come in.

Refrain:
Yes, Jesus loves me, Yes, Jesus loves me.
Yes, Jesus loves me, The Bible tells me so.

From *Little Ones Sing Praise* (1989 CPH), p. 42.

Jesus Lives!

BIBLE STORY

The Resurrection (Luke 24:1–12)

MATERIALS

Cornstarch "clay"

   2 parts table salt
   1 part cornstarch
   1 part water

Saucepan

Wooden spoon

Airtight container

Water in a bowl

Watercolor or tempera paint

Paintbrush

Acrylic spray (optional)

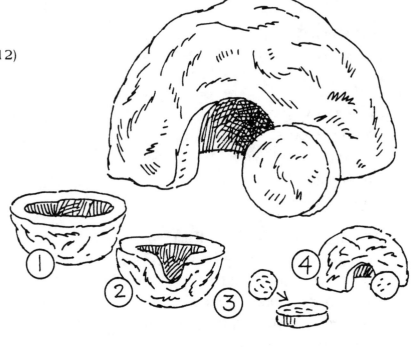

WAYS BIG HANDS CAN HELP

1. Mix together the ingredients for the cornstarch "clay" in a saucepan. Stir over low heat until stiff.

2. Divide up the clay, forming one ball for the demonstration and one for each child. Store in an airtight container until needed.

3. Show a ball of clay to the children. Talk about the joy that Jesus' friends felt when they found an empty tomb on the first Easter morning. Make the clay ball into the shape of an empty tomb. Demonstrate how to press into the center of the clay with your thumbs. Then pinch the ball into a cup shape by pushing the clay between your thumb and finger. Pinch off a "door" from the side of the cup. Roll and flatten it into a "stone" for the "doorway."

4. Set out a bowl of water for wetting the "stone" and sticking it to the side of the "tomb."

LITTLE FINGERS AT WORK

1. Take a few moments to experiment with your clay ball. See if you can press your thumb into the clay like your teacher did.

2. Pinch off a piece of clay from one side of the shape to make a doorway. Roll and flatten the ball of clay for the stone. Use water to stick it near the doorway of the tomb.

3. Put the "tomb" upside down and let it dry for two days.

4. Paint your model when dry and spray it with acrylic sealer (optional).

5. Rejoice that Jesus is risen!

Easter Garden

BIBLE STORY

The Resurrection (Luke 24:1–8)

MATERIALS

Construction paper (light blue and other assorted colors)

Glue

WAYS BIG HANDS CAN HELP

1. Tear construction paper of various colors into 2–3" pieces.

2. Set out glue and sheets of light blue construction paper.

3. Say, "How surprised the women were when they came to Jesus' tomb early Easter morning! How happy they were when two angels told them that Jesus was alive. Because Jesus lives, we can be happy too! We know that when we die, Jesus will someday make us alive again and take us to heaven to live with Him. Let's make a picture of Jesus' empty tomb in an Easter garden."

LITTLE HANDS AT WORK

1. Choose the colors of construction paper you want to use for your picture. Tear the paper into smaller pieces and shapes.

2. Glue the paper pieces onto the light blue paper to make an Easter garden. Let the picture remind you that Jesus, our Savior, lives!

OTHER IDEAS

1. Make an Easter flower garden from paper shapes.

2. Glue torn tissue-paper pieces onto construction paper. Brush with a mixture of white glue and water, in equal parts.

The Nets Were Full

BIBLE STORY

The Miraculous Catch of Fish (John 21:1–14)

MATERIALS

Stamp pad with ink

Light blue construction paper

Crayons

WAYS BIG HANDS CAN HELP

1. Set out glue, crayons, and paper. Provide a stamp pad for every 2–3 children.

2. Ask, "Have you ever tried really hard to do something, but still couldn't do it? Once Jesus' friends went fishing, and when they couldn't catch any fish, Jesus helped them. He used His power to fill their empty nets with many fish. As you draw a picture of this miracle, think about how Jesus has used His power to help you do something."

LITTLE HANDS AT WORK

1. Use a crayon to make both "up-and-down" and "side-to-side" lines on the paper for the "net."

2. Wet your fingertips on the stamp pad. Then make fingerprints over the net drawing. The crayon will resist the ink, creating the impression of fish behind the net. Wash your fingers well when you are done.

3. Use markers to draw eyes and fins on the fish.

4. Tell how Jesus uses His power to help you.

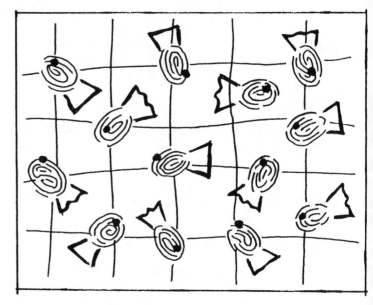

OTHER IDEAS

1. Make your own stamp pad. Fold two paper towels and put them on a paper plate. Pour liquid tempera paint over the towels, then add a little dishwashing liquid for easy cleanup.

2. Make your net by gluing pieces of yarn or vegetable netting to the paper.

3. Stamp on the net with the bottom of a plastic fruit basket dipped in tempera paint.

4. Have young children draw lines and fingerprint only. Omit details.

5. Use chocolate pudding or finger paint for stamping.

6. Draw a large fish outline and fingerprint "scales" on it.

7. Omit net. Make a fingerprint picture emphasizing God's creation of sea life, or add details to show other animals made by God.

Ascended into Heaven

BIBLE STORY

Jesus' Ascension (Acts 1:3–11)

MATERIALS

Blue poster board

Cloud dough

2 cups soap flakes

½ cup warm water

Mixing bowl

Electric mixer or rotary eggbeater

Crayons

WAYS BIG HANDS CAN HELP

1. Cut poster board in smaller sheets, one for each child. Set out crayons.

2. Enlarge, and cut out the Jesus pattern. Encourage older children to draw and cut out their own figure.

3. Mix soap flakes and water in a mixing bowl. Beat to the consistency of whipped cream.

4. Say, "Jesus' disciples watched as He rose into the clouds and went back to heaven. Jesus promises to come again someday and take us to live joyfully with Him forever. Let's make a picture to remind us of His promise."

5. Spoon some cloud dough on each child's sheet of poster board.

LITTLE FINGERS AT WORK

1. Use your fingers to make clouds from the dough.

2. Finish the drawing of Jesus and color it. Stick it onto the wet cloud dough.

OTHER IDEAS

1. Sprinkle several colors of powdered tempera paint onto the cloud dough.

2. Finger-paint the clouds and Jesus' picture.

3. Use commercial "sparkle" finger paints for a "heavenly" picture.

Flame of the Spirit

BIBLE STORY

Pentecost (Acts 2:1–41)

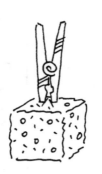

MATERIALS

Small sponge

Clip clothespin

Margarine tub

Red liquid tempera paint

Dishwashing liquid

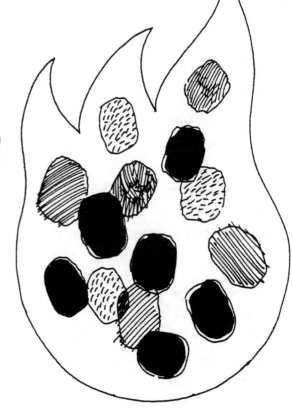

WAYS BIG HANDS CAN HELP

1. Draw a large flame shape for each child.

2. Pour red liquid tempera paint into margarine tubs, one tub for every two children. Add a little dishwashing liquid to the paint to aid in cleanup.

3. Clip a clothespin to the sponge.

4. Say, "God's Holy Spirit came with flames of fire at Pentecost. He filled many people with joy and excitement in knowing all about Jesus, our Savior. Let's make a sponge painting to remind us that God's Spirit comes to us today."

LITTLE HANDS AT WORK

1. Hold the clothespin and dip the sponge into the paint. Stamp the flame shape with color.

2. Show others your flame picture, and share the Good News about Jesus with them.

OTHER IDEAS

1. Pour red and yellow tempera paint into separate tubs. As the children paint their shape, let them discover how the colors mix together to make orange.

2. Stamp a burning bush shape like the one Moses saw.

3. Glue torn or crumpled pieces of red construction or tissue paper over the shape.

4. Paint the shape with a wide paintbrush or dab it with a sponge brush.

5. Let young children scribble over the shape.

6. Sprinkle glitter over the wet paint; the glitter will adhere to the paint as it dries.

7. Draw the heads of several disciples and stamp flames over them.

8. Encourage older children to draw and cut out their own flame shape.

9. Enlarge the flame pattern onto a large sheet of paper. Paint as a group project.